quick wreath designs

I0866988

hello

quick wreath designs

14 Projects to Make in an Afternoon

by Kim Wilson Byers

LEISURE ARTS
the art of everyday living

contents

introduction

Hey, friends! I'm thrilled you're joining me to learn how to make wreaths!

Wreaths aren't just for the front door anymore. We make wreaths for every room in the house. Where a picture once hung, now you'll find a wreath. What I love most about wreaths is their versatility. No matter what your personal style is—farmhouse or mid-century, modern or traditional, coastal or Victorian—you can make a wreath to match.

In this book, I'll show you how to make 14 different wreaths using multiple wreath forms—some common and easily found at your local craft store, some vintage and more likely found in grandma's attic. I'll walk you through the steps to make each one, with tips for customizing the designs through your color, floral, and fabric choices so you can make each project your own!

Let's get started!

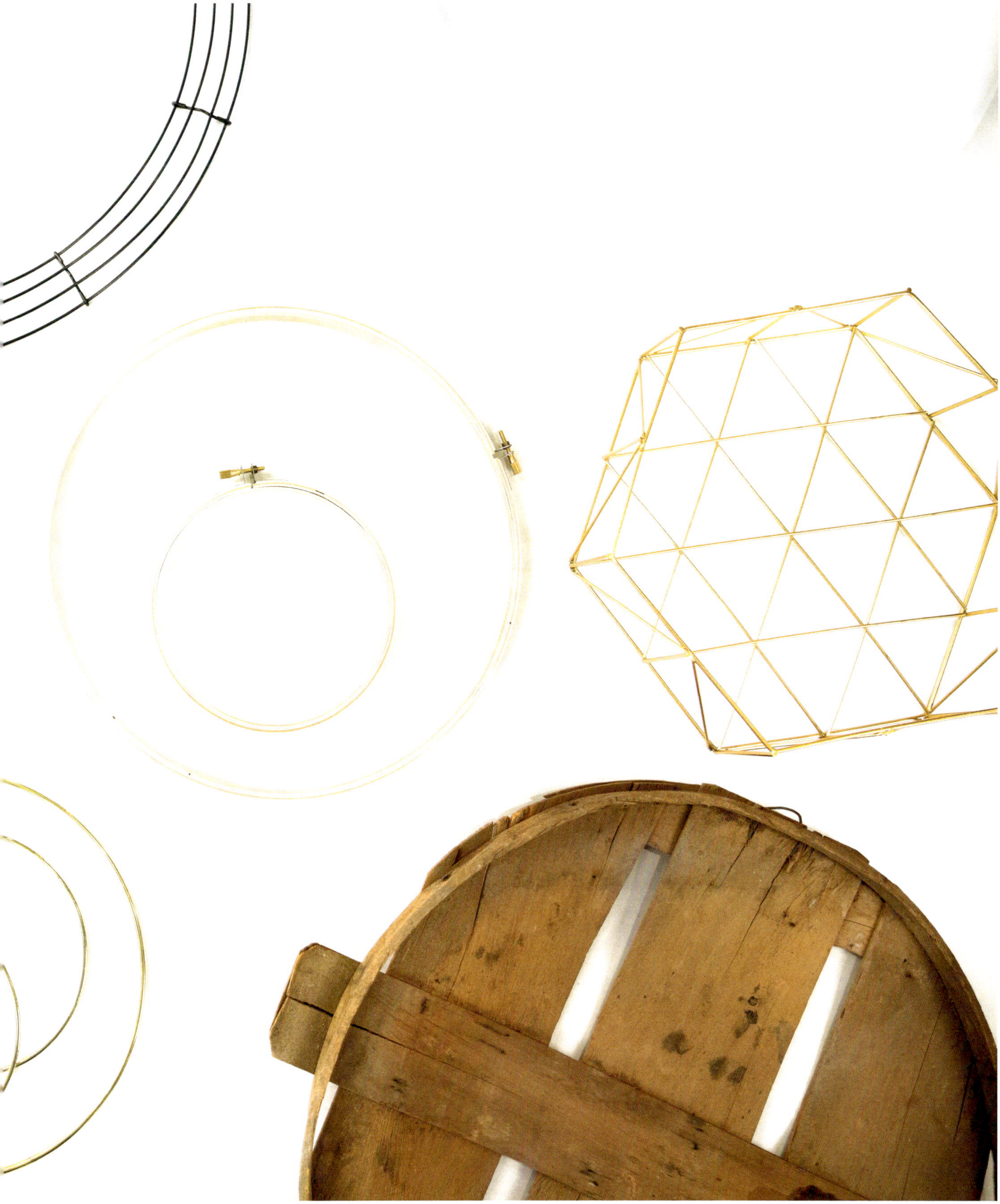

Meet Miss Boo Boo. She's a Shorkie and my sweet crafting companion. Boo sits with me while I design and follows me around while I work.

a bit about me

I'm a graphic designer, crafter, and all-around maker of things. It just feels good to make something that's entirely my own. Not every project turns out perfect the first time, but that's okay. For me, part of crafting is the experience of trying new things. It's a bit like therapy!

Where does your inspiration come from?

I developed a love for crafting from my mom and grandmother. My mom, Montia, has always had a knack for floral arranging and home décor, not to mention sewing. I can still learn a ton from her. My grandmother, Lou Ellen, made the most beautiful quilts. Her skill level was unmatched, in my opinion. Both of these women inspired me to craft, not for perfection, but for fun and a sense of accomplishment. Admittedly, I also like saving a dollar or two, so if I think I can make it for less, that's just what I do!

How did you get started designing?

I spent the first 10 years of my career as a Marketing VP at a major financial institution. Although marking mutual funds wasn't always exciting, it was an amazing career. Once my children were born, my priorities shifted, and I chose to leave that life and create something on my own that would allow me to spend more of my time with my boys. That was 11 years ago, and I've not looked back once. Graphic design of paper goods and craft supplies became the perfect creative outlet that allowed me to make a living and be present as my boys grew up.

What is your favorite color?

That's easy! My favorite color changes with the seasons. I'm in love with pink and light blue at Valentine's Day, yellow at Easter, red at the 4th of July, orange for Halloween and Thanksgiving, and silver and gold at Christmas!

What is your favorite craft?

Because I'm writing a wreath book, I suppose I should answer wreaths! Honestly, though, my favorite craft is a bit like my favorite color, it changes with the season. While I make wreaths year-round, my favorite times to make them are at Halloween and Christmas because I can get so very creative with the designs. I've made snake wreaths and bat wreaths at Halloween and snowmen wreaths and ornament wreaths at Christmas. It's so much fun! You can join me at *TheCelebrationShoppe.com* to see some of my designs.

What does your workspace look like?

In a word, messy! I'm always making something. That said, I do clean up between each craft by taking my space back down to white. Clearing away all the color helps me envision my next craft and keeps me from being distracted by what's left over from the last one. You can see a shot of my workspace above. If you want the full tour, check out the quick video I made on *TheCelebrationShoppe.com*.

Do you enjoy other hobbies outside of the craft room?

I've always loved the outdoors, especially hiking in our national and state parks. In 2018, my oldest son, Alex, started running cross country. I picked up the fever, as did my youngest son, Cole, and now we run almost daily. They outrun me by miles, literally. I can run four miles in the time they run seven or eight! But that's okay. It's been amazing, and it's nice to have something we can share.

getting started

I know you're excited about the best part, assembling your wreath. But before you get into the crafting, there are a few things you need to do first. To get started, you should think about where you want to hang your wreath, the type of form you'll use to make it, and the color or season that will inspire your design. Once you've done that, the hard part is over and all that's left is the fun!

Planning Your Design

There are a few things to consider when planning your wreath that will help you choose the materials you'll need for your design.

Where will you display your wreath?

If your wreath is going to be outside in the weather, avoid paper elements like floral paper on flower stems. Instead, choose exterior florals that will hold up in weather and sun.

How heavy will your wreath be?

Some wreaths, like my wagon wheel wreath on page 72, are very heavy. You'll need to hang heavy designs on a stud in your wall (usually 16 inches apart in most homes) or on an extra-strong doorhanger to support the weight.

How large can the wreath form be?

Measure the space where you want to hang your wreath, like between two windows, on a door, or above a mantel. Purchase a wreath form to fit the space, remembering that your florals or fabric may extend past the wreath form by 2 to 4 inches on all sides.

JUST ADD COLOR

To save on wreath forms and storage space, use a neutral wreath form as a base and simply change out the florals and other decorations as you move from season to season.

Choosing Your Color Palette

Color is everything. I often start with a color in mind, and when I get to the craft store, I select one item to build my wreath design around.

For instance, if I'm making a fall wreath and my color is orange, I find that one orange flower, floral spray, or fabric that will be the cornerstone of my design. And then I carry it around with me and use it to select all the other elements I'll use.

When selecting items, think of a color swatch at the paint store. Choose some things that are a few shades darker or lighter than your main color for coordinated variation.

Next, select complementary colors. For a fall wreath, I'd choose yellows and greens.

Gathering Your Materials

Now that you've considered your design and chosen your color palette, it's time to start choosing and gathering materials. There are loads of items you can use to make your wreath.

- Fabric
- Yarn
- Flowers
- Floral sprays
- Paper
- Felt
- Signs or letters

There are also many wreath form options, including straw, metal, vine, foam, and more. But not all wreath forms work well with all wreath materials. Here are some combinations of wreath forms and wreath-making materials that make good pairings.

- Wire wreath forms, some with multiple bands, are best paired with fabric strips and yarn.

- Straw wreath forms work great for fabrics and felt.

- Wooden embroidery hoops are perfect for yarn, fabrics, and all sorts of florals.

- Metal macramé hoops are perfect for yarn and greenery with florals.

- Vine wreath forms work very well with floral stems, large flowers, and ribbon.

There are also a number of non-traditional wreath forms that make beautiful statements. Things like metal planters, hula hoops, wagon wheels, bicycle spokes, colorful rainboots, and umbrellas! Pretty much anything that will hold greenery and flowers can be a wreath form!

Finally, don't forget about the tools you'll need to assemble your wreath. Depending on the wreath you're making and where it will hang, you'll need:

- Floral wire
- Floral tape
- Glue gun and hot glue
- Clear fishing line
- Floral snips

Once you've gathered everything you need for a project, lay out all of your tools and materials on your work surface. Personally, I like to start by placing materials on the wreath form in the approximate location I want them to be in the finished design so I can get an idea of how the finished wreath will look and make adjustments. Finally, it's time to start snipping, cutting, and securing your materials to your wreath form!